MUSICAL SELECTIONS

RAGS

The New American Musical

ISBN 0-634-05779-0

HAL•LEONARD® CORPORATION

7777 W. BLUEMOUND RD. P.O. BOX 13819 MILWAUKEE, WI 53213

In Australia Contact:
Hal Leonard Australia Pty. Ltd.
22 Taunton Drive P.O. Box 5130
Cheltenham East, 3192 Victoria, Australia
Email: ausadmin@halleonard.com

Visit Hal Leonard Online at
www.halleonard.com

CONTENTS

BLAME IT ON THE SUMMER NIGHT

Lyric by STEPHEN SCHWARTZ
Music by CHARLES STROUSE

Oh, it's way past time when I should be home in bed,

but I'm stand-ing here on this moon-lit street in-

stead. I want to drink the breeze in

and bathe in lan - tern light. Oh, my rea - son's gone and I

blame it on the sum - mer night. I see

cou - ples pass and their eyes are lu - mi - nous,

(Instrumental 2nd time...

let ring

BRAND NEW WORLD

Lyric by STEPHEN SCHWARTZ
Music by CHARLES STROUSE

CHILDREN OF THE WIND
(Show Version)

Lyric by STEPHEN SCHWARTZ
Music by CHARLES STROUSE

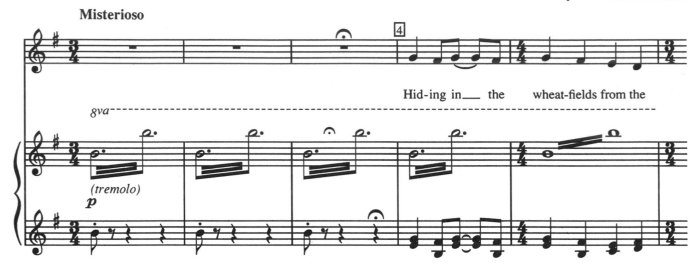

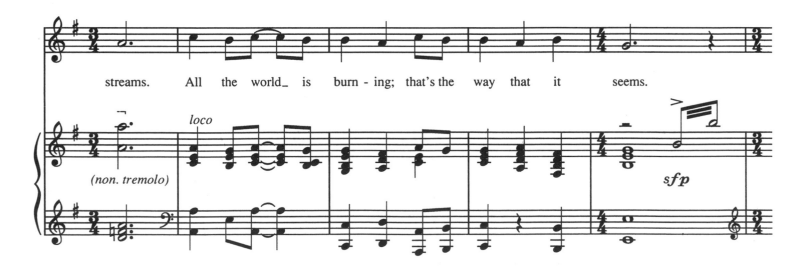

piec - es of the heart scat - tered worlds a -

part, so far from those we love,

all the chil - dren of the wind.

There's a morn-ing I want some - day to see;

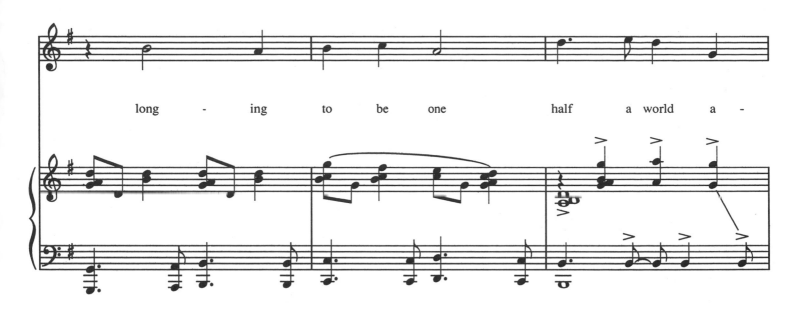

long - ing to be one half a world a -

way. We will make our way. Great

Maestoso

74

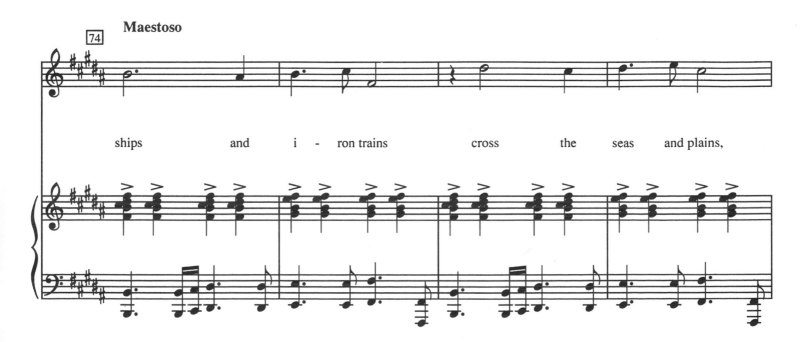

ships and i - ron trains cross the seas and plains,

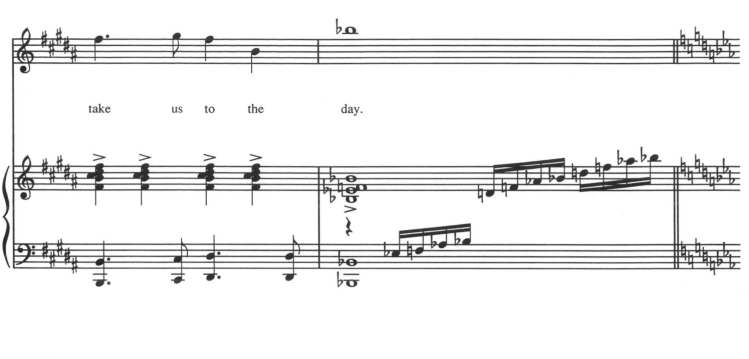

take us to the day.

Bring us to the shore, no more the chil - dren of the

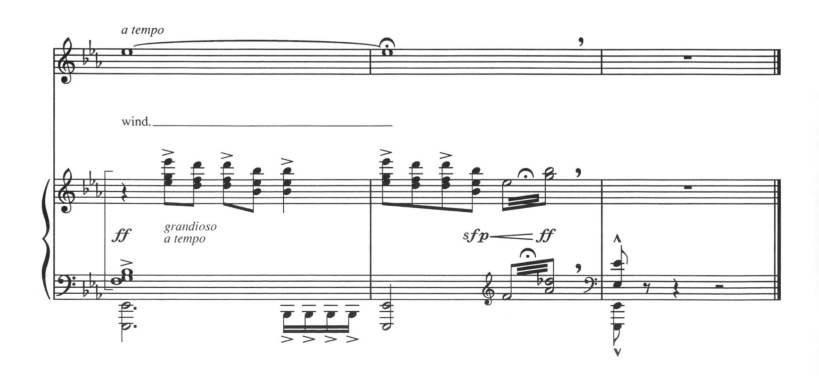

wind.

PENNY A TUNE

Lyric by STEPHEN SCHWARTZ
Music by CHARLES STROUSE

Pen-ny a tune, pen-ny a tune, tunes from a-round the block, tunes from a-far,

beau-ti-ful tunes played by mu-si-cians who played for the czar.

CHILDREN OF THE WIND
(Standard Version)

Lyric by STEPHEN SCHWARTZ
Music by CHARLES STROUSE

DANCING WITH THE FOOLS

Lyric by STEPHEN SCHWARTZ
Music by CHARLES STROUSE

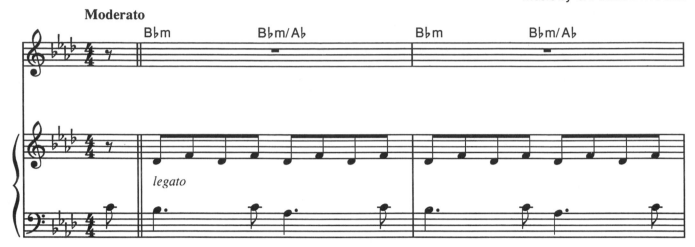

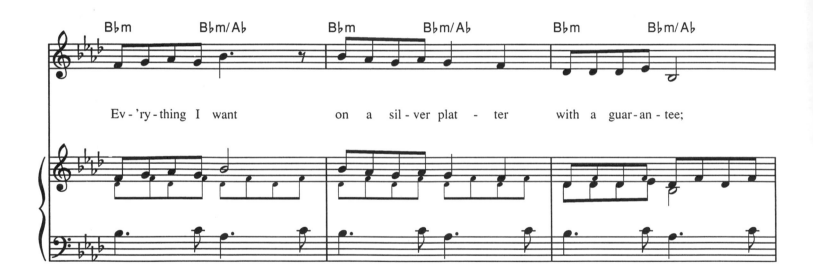

Ev - 'ry-thing I want on a sil - ver plat - ter with a guar-an - tee;

take his hand and go take___ it. What's the mat - ter?

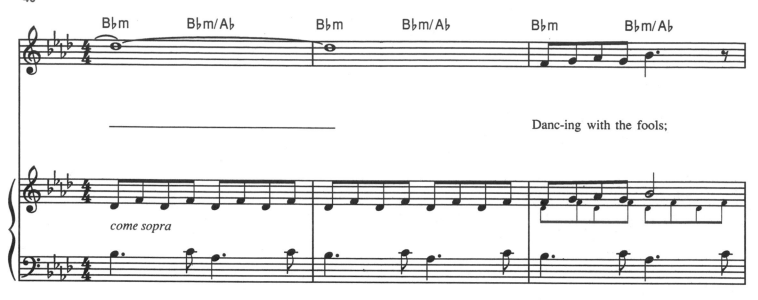

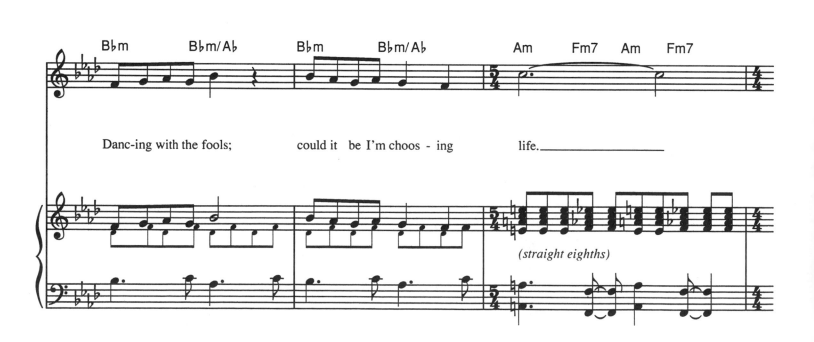

FOR MY MARY

Lyric by STEPHEN SCHWARTZ
Music by CHARLES STROUSE

Bowery waltz tempo

RAGS

Lyric by STEPHEN SCHWARTZ
Music by CHARLES STROUSE

Grandioso

Optional Coda

Here's where the beau - ty is, where the par - ty is. See that hand-some gent,

look how smart he is, danc - ing by in his fan - cy clothes. And he

sneers at me down his per - fect nose. And his hair is clean, and his

THREE SUNNY ROOMS

Lyric by STEPHEN SCHWARTZ
Music by CHARLES STROUSE

Easy 4 (conversationally)

WANTING

Lyric by STEPHEN SCHWARTZ
Music by CHARLES STROUSE

YANKEE BOY

Lyric by STEPHEN SCHWARTZ
Music by CHARLES STROUSE